Success FORMULA

$X = (TALK)^1 The + (Word^2) +$
$Y = (MEDITATE)^2 The + (Word^2) +$
$Z = (ACT+ON)^3 The + (Word^2) =$
Success!

GLORIA COPELAND

KENNETH
COPELAND
PUBLICATIONS

Unless otherwise noted, all scripture is from the *King James Version* of the Bible.

Scripture quotations marked *The Amplified Bible* are from *The Amplified Bible, Old Testament* © 1965, 1987. The Zondervan Corporation. © 1958, 1987 by The Lockman Foundation. Used by permission.

Scripture quotations marked *New International Version* are from *The Holy Bible, New International Version*®, © 1973, 1978, 1984 by International Bible Society. Used by permission of Zondervan Publishing House.

God's Success Formula

ISBN 0-88114-957-8   30-0532

10 09 08 07 06 05   11 10 9 8 7 6

© 1993 Eagle Mountain International Church, Inc. aka Kenneth Copeland Ministries

Kenneth Copeland Publications
Fort Worth, Texas 76192-0001
www.kcm.org

Printed in the United States of America. All rights reserved under International Copyright Law. No part of this book may be reproduced or transmitted in any form or by any means, electronic or mechanical, including photocopying, recording, or by any information storage and retrieval system, without the written permission of the publisher.

God's Success Formula
A Supernatural Success

May I ask you a very direct question? How much do you want to succeed in life?

Don't answer that too quickly. Obviously, no one aims to fail at anything they do. But I've been amazed over the years at the people who have come across the formula for success, only to leave it lying on the table while they stay broke, sick and defeated.

Such people initially think success is easy for those who are gifted with great abilities. When they run into the truth, however, it stops them cold. Because the reality is, real supernatural success is no picnic for anyone. It takes courage. It takes faith. And it doesn't have anything at all to do with natural ability.

If Joshua were around today, he could tell you just how true that is. When God called him to lead Israel after Moses' death, he faced an overwhelming task. As Moses' successor, Joshua had some big shoes to fill. Several million people were under his command, and he knew if they didn't stay in line with God, His blessing would not be on them. Without God's blessing, they would never be able to take the Promised Land.

Joshua had to succeed. The future of the entire nation was at stake. And succeed he did!

How did he do it? By following God's own formula for success.

If you're wishing God would give you such a formula—wish no more. He has. It's the same one He gave to Joshua and it will work just as well for you as it did for him.

Who's With You?

"But Gloria, you don't know *me!* I've tried and failed with every formula in the book. I just don't have what it takes to succeed."

If that's what you're thinking, you haven't tried the formula in God's Book. With His formula, you don't have to "have what it takes." Look at what God said in Joshua 1:5 and you'll see why: "There shall not any man be able to stand before thee all the days of thy life: as I was with Moses, *so I will be with thee: I will not fail thee, nor forsake thee*".

You may remember that God told Moses something very similar in the book of Exodus when Moses claimed he wasn't qualified to go before Pharaoh and demand Israel's freedom. He felt he was personally inadequate for the task. "Lord, who am I to go and do these things?" he said.

But God answered, "Certainly I will be with thee..." (Exodus 3:12). In other words, "It doesn't matter who you are, Moses. It matters who I am. For I am with you!"

That's the great thing about God's success formula. It's not based on our abilities, it's based on His abilities. We may be inadequate in a dozen different ways, but the One who is with us is more than enough.

An Act of Courage

Although it's great to know God is connected with you—that He never leaves you nor forsakes you—before He can release His power on your behalf, you have to be connected with

Him in return. You do this by obeying His Word. Joshua 1:7 says: "Only you be strong and very courageous, that you may do according to all the law which Moses My servant commanded you. Turn not from it to the right hand or to the left, that you may prosper wherever you go" (*The Amplified Bible*).

Do you know obeying the Word is an act of courage? Because when you obey the Word and believe God in a situation, you're swimming upstream. You're going against the current of the world.

When most of the people and all the circumstances around you are screaming unbelief in your ears, it takes courage to stand on God's Word and not be moved. But once you make the decision to do it, you'll be ready to activate God's three-part formula for success.

You'll find it spelled out in Joshua 1:8: "[1] This Book of the Law shall not depart out of your mouth, [2] but you shall meditate on it day and night, [3] that you may observe and do according to all that is written in it. For then you shall make your way prosperous, and then you shall deal wisely and have good success" (*The Amplified Bible*).

There they are. Three simple steps directly from the mouth of God. Steps that enabled Joshua to conquer the land of Canaan and bring Israel into their inheritance. Steps that will enable you to live like the conqueror God designed you to be.

Let's look at them one by one.

Success Step 1

"This Book of the Law shall not depart out of your mouth...." That's the first element of supernatural success God gives us in this verse. I like to say it this way: *Talk the Word.*

When I say talk the Word, I don't mean just every now and then when you're feeling spiritual. I mean continually. In Deuteronomy 6:7, God said you should talk His Word "when you sit at home and when you walk along the road, when you lie down and when you get up" (*New International Version*).

That's pretty much all the time, isn't it? At home, at work, in the grocery store—wherever you are, keep the Word of God in your mouth.

Romans 10:17 tells us that "faith cometh by hearing, and hearing by the word of God." So when you're continually talking about what God says, what He'll do and what His promises are, you're going to be growing in faith because you're hearing the Word from yourself all the time.

Some people find it hard to talk the Word that much. They just can't seem to do it! If you're one of them, let me tell you why that is.

Jesus said that out of the abundance of the heart the mouth speaketh (Luke 6:45). If you're focusing most of your attention on natural things—watching secular television, going to the movies, thinking about worldly matters, worrying about your job and family—then that's what is going to be in your heart in abundance. And that's what you're going to talk about.

To change what's coming out of your mouth, you must refocus your attention. Turn it toward God's Word and keep it there. Fill your heart with an abundance of the

Word and your mouth will get in line.

Success Step 2

This brings us to the second step of God's success formula. *"You shall meditate on it [the Word] day and night."*

When you meditate on God's Word, you do more than just read it. You take it into your heart in a very personal way and apply it to your own situation.

When you read a scripture about the blessing of prosperity, for example, don't think, *Hey, that sounds nice, but I could never have it.* Instead, apply it to yourself and say, "Hallelujah! That's God's Word to me. He says He'll meet my need liberally, according to His riches in glory by Christ Jesus and I'm expecting Him to do that in my situation!"

If you've been reading the Bible like a history book, make a change and begin to see it as God talking directly to you. Take time to meditate on it. Think about it. Digest it. Take it so personally that it moves from your head to your heart, and it will become powerful and active in your life.

Success Step 3

The final step of God's success formula involves action. *We must act as though the Word we've been talking and meditating is true—even when circumstances seem to say otherwise.*

If that puzzles you, read what Jesus said in Mark 11:22-24:

> Have faith in God. For verily I say unto you, That whosoever shall say unto this mountain, Be thou removed, and be thou cast into the sea; and shall not doubt in his heart, but shall believe that those things which he saith shall come to pass; he shall have whatsoever he saith. Therefore I say unto you, What things soever ye desire, when ye pray, believe that ye receive them, and ye shall have them.

Notice Jesus didn't say you should believe you receive when you see it. He said to believe you receive when you pray.

Now, if you follow His instructions, how do you think you should act? Should you walk around depressed and joyless? Should you stand around wringing your hands, worrying?

No! Rejoice and praise God for the answer to your prayer. Act like you've already received it.

Right here is where many people miss it. They know God's Word works, but they fail to act on it.

You may have been studying the Word for 20 years. You may know how to live by faith better than anyone around. But, remember, it's not what you know that will bring you through in victory—it's what you do.

You can walk in faith consistently through 10 trials that come your way and experience great success. Yet on the 11th one, if you neglect to act on the Word, you'll fail. Although the string of victories in your past is a wonderful thing, it's what you do today that will get you through today's test or trial.

More Than Mental Assent

One of the greatest enemies of real faith is a thing I call "mental assent." People who operate in mental assent read the Word and think they believe it, but when pressure comes, they don't act it.

Mental assent says, "I believe the Bible from cover to cover. I believe I'm healed by the stripes of Jesus because the Bible says so." But when sickness actually attacks, it stops saying, "By His stripes I'm healed" and starts saying, "I'm sick."

Real faith believes what the Word says even though sight and feelings say something different. Faith doesn't care what the symptoms are. It doesn't care what the circumstances look like. It's not moved by what the banker, or the doctor, or the lawyer, or the bill collector says.

Faith in God's Word will change the symptoms. It will change the bank account. It will bring the money to get the bills paid.

Faith will turn every defeat into victory. It *is* God's success formula!

But you have to give that faith an opportunity to work. You have to keep God's Word in your mouth and meditate on it in your heart "that you may observe to do according to all that is written in it. For then you shall make your way prosperous, and then you shall deal wisely and have good success."

No Sorrow Included

Now, think again about that question I asked you earlier. How much do you want to succeed in life? Enough to change what you're saying? Enough to change where your attention is focused? Enough to act on the Word of God even when the rest of the world is telling you it will never work?

If you want it that much, the Word of God guarantees you'll get your fill of success in life. Good success. Not the kind the world gives, but God's own brand of success.

Success the world's way has a price tag of misery attached to it. But Proverbs 10:22 says,

"The blessing of the Lord, it maketh rich, and he addeth no sorrow with it."

I will warn you that Satan won't like it if you choose the way of success. He'll do whatever he can to stop you, and since he knows God's success formula, he knows exactly what tactics to use.

He'll pressure you to say negative things. He'll try to distract you from the Word and get your attention on anything—it doesn't matter what it is—as long as it isn't the Word.

His goal is to stop your faith. He knows it's the only force that can cause impossible situations to change.

He also knows that it comes from the Word of God. So when he sees that Word going in your heart and hears it coming out of your mouth, he doesn't just sit there. He starts talking. Doubtful thoughts will begin to come into your mind—thoughts that are just the opposite of what God's Word says.

But those thoughts don't become yours unless you believe them and speak them. That's what he wants you to do, of course. If the Word says you're healed, he'll tell you you're sick. If the Word says you're forgiven, he'll say you're still guilty. If the Word says your needs are met, he'll tell you they're not.

But if you won't let go, if you keep the Word in your mouth and in your heart, you can't lose. There's no force the devil can bring against you that will overcome the Word of God. It will make you a winner every time.

So if you've been wanting good success and it's been eluding you, quit wondering if you have what it takes to make it—and remember instead who is with you. Then turn to the Word of God and put God's success formula to work in your life. Start talking it. Start thinking it. Start doing it.

Before long, you won't be chasing success...it will be chasing you!

Prayer for Salvation and Baptism in the Holy Spirit

Heavenly Father, I come to You in the Name of Jesus. Your Word says, "Whosoever shall call on the name of the Lord shall be saved" (Acts 2:21). I am calling on You. I pray and ask Jesus to come into my heart and be Lord over my life according to Romans 10:9-10: "If thou shalt confess with thy mouth the Lord Jesus, and shalt believe in thine heart that God hath raised him from the dead, thou shalt be saved. For with the heart man believeth unto righteousness; and with the mouth confession is made unto salvation." I do that now. I confess that Jesus is Lord, and I believe in my heart that God raised Him from the dead.

I am now reborn! I am a Christian—a child of Almighty God! I am saved! You also said in Your Word, "If ye then, being evil, know how to give good gifts unto your children: HOW MUCH MORE shall your heavenly Father give the Holy Spirit to them that ask him?" (Luke 11:13). I'm also asking You to fill me with the Holy Spirit. Holy Spirit, rise up within me as I praise God. I fully expect to speak with other tongues as You give me the utterance (Acts 2:4). In Jesus' Name. Amen!

Begin to praise God for filling you with the Holy Spirit. Speak those words and syllables you receive—not in your own language, but the language given to you by the Holy Spirit. You have to use your own voice. God will not force you to speak. Don't be concerned with how it sounds. It is a heavenly language!

Continue with the blessing God has given you and pray in the spirit every day.

You are a born-again, Spirit-filled believer. You'll never be the same!

Find a good church that boldly preaches God's Word and obeys it. Become a part of a church family who will love and care for you as you love and care for them.

We need to be connected to each other. It increases our strength in God. It's God's plan for us.

Make it a habit to watch the *Believer's Voice of Victory* television broadcast and become a doer of the Word, who is blessed in his doing (James 1:22-25).

About the Author

Gloria Copeland is a noted author and minister of the gospel whose teaching ministry is known throughout the world. Believers worldwide know her through Believers' Conventions, Victory Campaigns, magazine articles, teaching audios and videos, and the daily and Sunday *Believer's Voice of Victory* television broadcast, which she hosts with her husband, Kenneth Copeland. She is known for "Healing School," which she began teaching and hosting in 1979 at KCM meetings. Gloria delivers the Word of God and the keys to victorious Christian living to millions of people every year.

Gloria has written many books, including *God's Will for You, Walk With God, God's Will Is Prosperity, Hidden Treasures, Living Contact* and *Are You Listening?* She has also co-authored several books with her husband, including *Family Promises, Healing Promises* and the best-selling daily devotionals, *From Faith to Faith* and *Pursuit of His Presence*.

She holds an honorary doctorate from Oral Roberts University. In 1994, Gloria was voted Christian Woman of the Year, an honor conferred on women whose example demonstrates outstanding Christian leadership. Gloria is also the co-founder and vice president of Kenneth Copeland Ministries in Fort Worth, Texas.

Learn more about
Kenneth Copeland Ministries
by visiting our Web site
at **www.kcm.org**

Materials to Help You Receive Your Healing
by Gloria Copeland

Books

* And Jesus Healed Them All
  God's Prescription for Divine Health
* Harvest of Health
  Words That Heal (gift book with CD enclosed)

Audio Resources

God Is a Good God
God Wants You Well
Healing School

Video Resources

Healing School: God Wants You Well
Know Him as Healer

DVD Resources
Be Made Whole—Live Long, Live Healthy

*Available in Spanish

Books Available From Kenneth Copeland Ministries

by Kenneth Copeland

*   A Ceremony of Marriage
     A Matter of Choice
     Covenant of Blood
     Faith and Patience—The Power Twins
*   Freedom From Fear
     Giving and Receiving
     Honor—Walking in Honesty, Truth and Integrity
     How to Conquer Strife
     How to Discipline Your Flesh
     How to Receive Communion
     In Love There Is No Fear
     Know Your Enemy
     Living at the End of Time—A Time of Supernatural Increase
     Love Never Fails
     Managing God's Mutual Funds—Yours and His
     Mercy—The Divine Rescue of the Human Race
*   Now Are We in Christ Jesus
     One Nation Under God (gift book with CD enclosed)
*   Our Covenant With God
     Partnership, Sharing the Vision—Sharing the Grace
*   Prayer—Your Foundation for Success
*   Prosperity: The Choice Is Yours
     Rumors of War
*   Sensitivity of Heart
*   Six Steps to Excellence in Ministry
*   Sorrow Not! Winning Over Grief and Sorrow

- * The Decision Is Yours
- * The Force of Faith
- * The Force of Righteousness
- The Image of God in You
- * The Laws of Prosperity
- * The Mercy of God (available in Spanish only)
- The Outpouring of the Spirit—The Result of Prayer
- * The Power of the Tongue
- The Power to Be Forever Free
- * The Winning Attitude
- Turn Your Hurts Into Harvests
- Walking in the Realm of the Miraculous
- * Welcome to the Family
- * You Are Healed!
- Your Right-Standing With God

by Gloria Copeland

- * And Jesus Healed Them All
- Are You Listening?
- Are You Ready?
- Be a Vessel of Honor
- Blessed Beyond Measure
- Build Your Financial Foundation
- Fight On!
- Go With the Flow
- God's Prescription for Divine Health
- God's Success Formula
- God's Will for You
- God's Will for Your Healing
- God's Will Is Prosperity
- * God's Will Is the Holy Spirit
- * Harvest of Health

*Available in Spanish

Hidden Treasures
Living Contact
Living in Heaven's Blessings Now
Looking for a Receiver
* Love—The Secret to Your Success
No Deposit—No Return
Pleasing the Father
Pressing In—It's Worth It All
Shine On!
The Grace That Makes Us Holy
The Power to Live a New Life
The Protection of Angels
There Is No High Like the Most High
The Secret Place of God's Protection (gift book with CD enclosed)
The Unbeatable Spirit of Faith
This Same Jesus
To Know Him
* Walk in the Spirit (available in Spanish only)
Walk With God
Well Worth the Wait
Words That Heal (gift book with CD enclosed)
Your Promise of Protection—The Power of the 91st Psalm

Books Co-Authored by Kenneth and Gloria Copeland

Family Promises
Healing Promises
Prosperity Promises
Protection Promises

* From Faith to Faith—A Daily Guide to Victory
From Faith to Faith—A Perpetual Calendar

One Word From God Can Change Your Life

One Word From God Series:
- One Word From God Can Change Your Destiny
- One Word From God Can Change Your Family
- One Word From God Can Change Your Finances
- One Word From God Can Change Your Formula for Success
- One Word From God Can Change Your Health
- One Word From God Can Change Your Nation
- One Word From God Can Change Your Prayer Life
- One Word From God Can Change Your Relationships

Load Up—A Youth Devotional
Over the Edge—A Youth Devotional
Pursuit of His Presence—A Daily Devotional
Pursuit of His Presence—A Perpetual Calendar
Raising Children Without Fear

Other Books Published by KCP

The First 30 Years—A Journey of Faith
   The story of the lives of Kenneth and Gloria Copeland
Real People. Real Needs. Real Victories.
   A book of testimonies to encourage your faith
John G. Lake—His Life, His Sermons, His Boldness of Faith
The Holiest of All by Andrew Murray
The New Testament in Modern Speech by
   Richard Francis Weymouth
The Rabbi From Burbank by Rabbi Isidor Zwirn and
   Bob Owen
Unchained! by Mac Gober

*Available in Spanish

Products Designed for Today's Children and Youth

And Jesus Healed Them All (confession book and CD gift package)
Baby Praise Board Book
Baby Praise Christmas Board Book
Noah's Ark Coloring Book
The Best of *Shout!* Adventure Comics
The *Shout!* Giant Flip Coloring Book
The *Shout!* Joke Book
The *Shout!* Super-Activity Book
Wichita Slim's Campfire Stories

*Commander Kellie and the Superkids*_{SM} Books:

The SWORD Adventure Book
*Commander Kellie and the Superkids*_{SM}
  Solve-It-Yourself Mysteries
*Commander Kellie and the Superkids*_{SM} Adventure Series:
  Middle Grade Novels by Christopher P.N. Maselli:

   #1 The Mysterious Presence
   #2 The Quest for the Second Half
   #3 Escape From Jungle Island
   #4 In Pursuit of the Enemy
   #5 Caged Rivalry
   #6 Mystery of the Missing Junk
   #7 Out of Breath
   #8 The Year Mashela Stole Christmas
   #9 False Identity
   #10 The Runaway Mission
   #11 The Knight-Time Rescue of Commander Kellie

World Offices
of Kenneth Copeland Ministries

For more information about KCM and a free
catalog, please write the office nearest you:

Kenneth Copeland Ministries
Fort Worth, Texas 76192-0001

Kenneth Copeland
Locked Bag 2600
Mansfield Delivery Centre
QUEENSLAND 4122
AUSTRALIA

Kenneth Copeland
Post Office Box 15
BATH
BA1 3XN
U.K.

Kenneth Copeland

Private Bag X 909
FONTAINEBLEAU
2032
REPUBLIC OF
SOUTH AFRICA

Kenneth Copeland
Ministries
PO Box 3111 STN LCD 1
Langley B.C V3A 4R3
CANADA

Kenneth Copeland Ministries
Post Office Box 84
L'VIV 79000
UKRAINE

JESUS IS LORD

We're Here for You!

Believer's Voice of Victory Television Broadcast

Join Kenneth and Gloria Copeland and the *Believer's Voice of Victory* broadcasts Monday through Friday and on Sunday each week, and learn how faith in God's Word can take your life from ordinary to extraordinary. This teaching from God's Word is designed to get you where you want to be—*on top!*

You can catch the *Believer's Voice of Victory* broadcast on your local, cable or satellite channels.

Check your local listings for times and stations in your area.

Believer's Voice of Victory Magazine

Enjoy inspired teaching and encouragement from Kenneth and Gloria Copeland and guest ministers each month in the *Believer's Voice of Victory* magazine. Also included are real-life testimonies of God's miraculous power and divine intervention in the lives of people just like you!

It's more than just a magazine—it's a ministry.

To receive a FREE subscription to *Believer's Voice of Victory*, write to:

Kenneth Copeland Ministries
Fort Worth, Texas 76192-0001
Or call:
(800) 600-7395
(7 a.m.-5 p.m. CT)
Or visit our Web site at:
www.kcm.org

If you are writing from outside the U.S., please contact the KCM office nearest you. Addresses for all Kenneth Copeland Ministries offices are listed on the previous pages.